Social Media Monetization Handbook

Leveraging Your Online Presence to Turn Likes and Followers into Income

Carl Robson

Social Media Monetization Handbook
© Copyright 2023 by Carl Robson
All rights reserved

This document is geared towards providing exact and reliable information with regards to the topic and issue covered. The publication is sold with the idea that the publisher is not required to render accounting, officially permitted, or otherwise, qualified services. If advice is necessary, legal or professional, a practiced individual in the profession should be ordered.

From a Declaration of Principles which was accepted and approved equally by a Committee of the American Bar Association and a Committee of Publishers and Associations.

In no way is it legal to reproduce, duplicate, or transmit any part of this document in either electronic means or in printed format. Recording of this publication is strictly prohibited and any storage of this document is not allowed unless with written permission from the publisher. All rights reserved.

The information provided herein is stated to be truthful and consistent, in that any liability, in terms of inattention or otherwise, by any usage or abuse of any policies, processes, or directions contained within is the solitary and utter responsibility of the recipient reader. Under no circumstances will any legal responsibility or blame be held against the publisher for any reparation, damages, or monetary loss due to the information herein, either directly or indirectly.

Respective authors own all copyrights not held by the publisher.

The information herein is offered for informational purposes solely, and is universal as so. The presentation of the information is without contract or any type of guarantee assurance.

The trademarks that are used are without any consent, and the publication of the trademark is without permission or backing by the trademark owner. All trademarks and brands within this book are for clarifying purposes only and are owned by the owners themselves, not affiliated with this document.

TABLE OF CONTENTS

Chapter 1: Introduction to Social Media Monetization

Chapter 2: Building a Solid Online Presence

Chapter 3: Developing a Monetization Strategy

Chapter 4: Mastering Social Media Algorithms

Chapter 5: Growing Your Follower Base

Chapter 6: Monetizing Content through Ads

Chapter 7: Harnessing the Power of Affiliate Marketing

Chapter 8: Securing Lucrative Sponsorships

Chapter 9: Diversifying Income Streams

Chapter 10: Legal and Ethical Considerations

Chapter 11: Overcoming Challenges in Social Media Monetization

Chapter 12: Future Trends in Social Media Monetization

Chapter 1: Introduction to Social Media Monetization

In the fast-paced digital age, social media has become more than just a platform for sharing photos and staying connected with friends. It has evolved into a powerful tool for individuals and businesses alike to leverage their online presence and turn likes and followers into a sustainable income. This chapter serves as a foundational guide, laying the groundwork for understanding the landscape of social media monetization, exploring its evolution, and establishing realistic goals and expectations for those embarking on this exciting journey.

1.1 Understanding the Landscape of Social Media

Social media platforms are diverse ecosystems, each with its unique features, audience demographics, and content preferences. To effectively navigate the landscape of social media monetization, it's crucial to comprehend the dynamics of popular platforms such as Instagram, Facebook, TikTok, YouTube, and Twitter.

Niche Identification and Target Audience

Begin by identifying your niche – the specific area or topic that aligns with your passion and expertise. Whether it's fashion, gaming, lifestyle, or technology, understanding your niche helps in tailoring content that resonates with a particular audience. Research your target audience's preferences, behaviors, and trends relevant to your chosen niche.

Content Creation and Engagement

Successful social media monetization hinges on the creation of high-quality, engaging content. Develop a content strategy that aligns with your niche and captivates your audience. Utilize a mix of photos, videos, and interactive elements to keep your followers entertained and invested in your online presence. Engagement is key; respond to comments, ask questions, and foster a sense of community around your content.

Platform-Specific Strategies

Different platforms require different strategies. Instagram thrives on visually appealing images and stories, while Twitter demands concise and impactful messages. Tailor your approach to each platform to maximize your reach and engagement. Stay informed about platform algorithm changes, trends, and best practices to adapt your strategy accordingly.

1.2 The Evolution of Social Media Monetization

The landscape of social media monetization is in a constant state of evolution, shaped by technological advancements, cultural shifts, and user behavior. Understanding this evolution is crucial for staying ahead of the curve and capitalizing on emerging opportunities.

Early Monetization Efforts

In the early days of social media, monetization was limited to brand partnerships and sponsored posts. Influencers collaborated with brands, promoting products to their audience in exchange for compensation. While effective, these partnerships were often informal and lacked the structure seen in today's sophisticated influencer marketing landscape.

Rise of Ad-based Monetization

As social media platforms matured, they introduced ad-based monetization models. Facebook, Instagram, and YouTube, among others, integrated advertising features, allowing content creators to earn revenue based on ad views and clicks. Understanding the nuances of each platform's ad system became essential for maximizing earnings.

Diversification of Monetization Streams

The evolution continues with influencers diversifying their income streams. Beyond ads, monetization now includes affiliate marketing, sponsored content, e-commerce, and exclusive memberships. This diversification not only provides more revenue opportunities but also insulates influencers from fluctuations in a single income source.

1.3 Setting Your Goals and Expectations

Before embarking on the journey of social media monetization, it's crucial to establish clear goals and realistic expectations. While the allure of quick success and financial gains is present, a thoughtful approach will lead to sustainable, long-term success.

Defining Your Objectives

Ask yourself: What do you want to achieve through social media monetization? Is it financial independence, brand recognition, or the ability to influence and inspire others? Clearly defining your objectives will shape your strategy and guide your decision-making throughout the monetization process.

Realistic Timeframes and Milestones

Monetizing your online presence is not an overnight success story. Set realistic timeframes and milestones, understanding that building a substantial following and establishing profitable partnerships takes time. Patience and persistence are key virtues in this dynamic landscape.

Metrics for Success

Identify key performance indicators (KPIs) that align with your goals. Whether it's follower growth, engagement rates, or revenue generated, tracking metrics will help you assess the effectiveness of your strategies. Regularly evaluate your performance and adjust your approach based on the insights gained.

In conclusion, the landscape of social media monetization is vast and dynamic. By understanding the nuances of different platforms, recognizing the evolution of monetization strategies, and setting realistic goals, you lay a solid foundation for a successful journey into turning your online presence into a lucrative income stream. The chapters that follow will delve deeper into the specific strategies and tactics that will empower you to thrive in this exciting and ever-changing digital landscape.

Chapter 2: Building a Solid Online Presence

In the world of social media monetization, a strong and distinctive online presence is the cornerstone of success. This chapter explores the fundamental elements of building a solid online presence, with a focus on crafting an engaging personal brand, strategically choosing platforms, and creating high-quality content that resonates with your audience.

2.1 Crafting an Engaging Personal Brand

Your personal brand is the essence of who you are on social media – it's your identity, values, and the unique qualities that set you apart. Crafting an engaging personal brand is not just about aesthetics;

it's about creating a narrative that captivates and resonates with your target audience.

Authenticity and Consistency

Authenticity is the bedrock of a compelling personal brand. Be genuine, transparent, and true to yourself. Consistency in your messaging, visual elements, and tone helps build trust and familiarity with your audience. Whether you're quirky, informative, or inspirational, let your brand voice shine through consistently.

Visual Identity

The visual elements of your personal brand, including your profile picture, color scheme, and overall aesthetic, should align with your chosen niche and resonate with your audience. Consider creating a recognizable logo or watermark to enhance brand visibility across platforms. A cohesive visual identity strengthens brand recall.

Storytelling and Narrative

Craft a compelling narrative that tells the story of your journey, values, and aspirations. Share personal anecdotes, triumphs, and challenges to create a connection with your audience. A well-told story not only engages but also humanizes your online presence, making you relatable and memorable.

2.2 Choosing the Right Platforms for Your Niche

Not all social media platforms are created equal, and choosing the right ones for your niche is crucial for effective online presence. Different platforms cater to distinct demographics and content preferences, so strategic selection ensures that your efforts are focused where they will have the most impact.

Audience Demographics

Research the demographics of each platform to align with your target audience. For instance, Instagram may be ideal for visual-centric content and a younger demographic, while LinkedIn might suit a more professional and business-oriented audience. Understanding these nuances helps you tailor your content for maximum resonance.

Platform-Specific Features

Each platform offers unique features and tools. Consider the format of content each platform prioritizes — whether it's images, videos, short-form content, or long-form articles. Leverage platform-specific features such as Instagram Stories, YouTube Shorts, or Twitter Fleets to enhance engagement and visibility.

Cross-Platform Consistency

While choosing platforms strategically, maintain a consistent brand presence across them. Use the same profile picture, handle, and visual elements to create a cohesive experience for followers who may engage with you on multiple platforms. Consistency reinforces brand recognition and builds a unified online identity.

2.3 Creating High-Quality Content that Resonates

Compelling content is the driving force behind a solid online presence. To capture and retain the attention of your audience, focus on creating content that is not only visually appealing but also adds value, entertains, or educates.

Understanding Your Audience's Needs

Research your audience's preferences, pain points, and interests. Tailor your content to address these needs, whether it's providing informative how-to guides, entertaining storytelling, or inspirational messages. By understanding your audience, you can create content that resonates and fosters a stronger connection.

Visual Excellence

Invest time and effort into the visual aspects of your content. High-quality images, well-edited videos, and aesthetically pleasing designs contribute to a professional and engaging feed. Utilize tools and apps for photo and video editing to enhance the visual appeal of your content.

Consistent Posting Schedule

Consistency in your posting schedule is vital for maintaining audience engagement. Whether you post daily, several times a week, or follow a specific schedule, let your audience know when to expect new content. Consistency builds anticipation and keeps your brand at the forefront of your followers' minds.

Engagement and Interaction

Encourage engagement by responding to comments, asking questions, and conducting polls or surveys. Actively participate in conversations within your niche and respond to direct messages. This not only builds a sense of community around your brand but also signals to algorithms that your content is worth promoting.

In conclusion, building a solid online presence requires intentional efforts in crafting an engaging personal brand, selecting the right platforms for your niche, and consistently creating high-quality content. As you navigate these aspects, keep in mind that authenticity, strategic choices, and meaningful engagement with your audience are the keys to not only attracting followers but also converting that attention into a monetizable online presence.

Chapter 3: Developing a Monetization Strategy

In the ever-evolving landscape of social media, turning your online presence into a lucrative income stream requires a well-defined monetization strategy. This chapter dives into the intricacies of developing a strategy that aligns with your goals, emphasizing the importance of identifying your target audience, exploring diverse monetization models such as ads, affiliate marketing, and sponsorships, and finding the delicate balance between authenticity and profitability.

3.1 Identifying Your Target Audience
Understanding your target audience is the linchpin of any successful monetization strategy. Your audience is not just a number of followers; they are individuals

with specific interests, preferences, and behaviors. By delving deep into their characteristics, you can tailor your content and monetization efforts more effectively.

Audience Persona Development

Create detailed audience personas by considering demographic information, interests, and challenges. Understand the problems your audience faces and how your content or products can provide solutions. Knowing your audience on a personal level allows you to create content that resonates and build a more engaged community.

Analyzing Audience Analytics

Leverage analytics tools provided by social media platforms to gain insights into your audience's demographics, engagement patterns, and content preferences. Track metrics such as age, location, and the times your audience is most active. This data guides your content strategy and helps you identify opportunities for monetization that align with your audience's interests.

Audience Feedback and Surveys

Directly engage with your audience through comments, polls, and surveys. Encourage feedback about your content and their preferences. By actively involving your audience in decisions, you not only strengthen the community aspect but also gather valuable insights for refining your monetization strategy.

3.2 Exploring Monetization Models: Ads, Affiliate Marketing, and Sponsorships

Diversifying your income streams is crucial for building a sustainable monetization strategy. Explore various models that align with your content and audience, including ads, affiliate marketing, and sponsorships.

Ads: Leveraging Platform Advertising

Platform-based advertising, such as Instagram Ads or YouTube AdSense, allows you to earn revenue based on ad views and clicks. Understand the ad policies of each platform and optimize your content to maximize ad revenue. Striking a balance between sponsored content and organic posts maintains a positive user experience.

Affiliate Marketing: Partnering for Profit

Affiliate marketing involves promoting products or services and earning a commission for every sale generated through your unique affiliate link. Identify affiliate programs relevant to your niche and audience. Disclose your affiliate relationships transparently to maintain trust and credibility with your followers.

Sponsorships: Building Strategic Partnerships

Sponsorships involve collaborating with brands for mutual benefit. Approach brands that align with your values and resonate with your audience. Craft compelling sponsorship proposals showcasing your reach, engagement, and the value you can provide to the brand. Clearly define the terms of the partnership to ensure a win-win scenario.

3.3 Balancing Authenticity and Profitability

Maintaining authenticity is paramount as you embark on the journey of monetizing your social media presence. Building trust with your audience is a long-term investment, and striking the right balance between authenticity and profitability is key.

Selecting Partnerships Wisely

When considering partnerships, choose brands and products that genuinely align with your values and resonate with your audience. Promoting products solely for financial gain, without consideration for your audience's needs, can erode trust. Prioritize authenticity over short-term financial gains.

Integrating Ads Seamlessly

If you choose to include ads in your monetization strategy, integrate them seamlessly into your content.

Avoid disruptive or intrusive ads that detract from the user experience. Select brands and products that align with your brand identity, ensuring a cohesive and authentic content flow.

Transparent Communication

Maintain transparent communication with your audience regarding sponsored content, affiliate links, and partnerships. Clearly disclose your relationships with brands, and emphasize the value or relevance of the promoted products. Honesty fosters trust, and an informed audience is more likely to support your monetization efforts.

Consistency in Brand Voice

Consistency in your brand voice is crucial for balancing authenticity and profitability. Whether you're creating sponsored content, affiliate promotions, or organic posts, maintain a consistent tone and messaging. This ensures that your audience recognizes and trusts your brand identity across all monetization efforts.

In conclusion, developing a monetization strategy involves a deep understanding of your target audience, exploration of diverse monetization models, and a delicate balance between authenticity and profitability. As you navigate the complexities of turning your online presence into income, remember that a well-crafted strategy, aligned with your audience's needs and your brand values, sets the foundation for sustainable success.

Chapter 4: Mastering Social Media Algorithms

In the intricate world of social media, mastering algorithms is the key to unlocking increased visibility, engagement, and ultimately, successful monetization. This chapter delves into the nuances of navigating social media algorithms, including decoding changes and updates, leveraging algorithmic trends, and maximizing reach and engagement for content creators aiming to turn their online presence into a lucrative income stream.

4.1 Decoding Algorithm Changes and Updates

Social media platforms regularly update and tweak their algorithms, impacting how content is displayed to users. Staying informed about these changes is crucial for content creators seeking to optimize their strategies and maintain visibility.

Platform-Specific Updates

Different platforms have unique algorithms, and understanding updates on platforms such as Instagram, Facebook, Twitter, and TikTok is essential. Subscribe to official platform blogs, attend webinars, and follow industry experts to stay abreast of changes. These updates can range from alterations in content prioritization to changes in engagement metrics.

Impact on Content Visibility

Algorithm changes often influence how content appears on users' feeds. For instance, a platform might prioritize video content over images or favor posts from accounts with higher engagement rates. Understanding these shifts allows content creators to adapt their content strategy to align with the current algorithmic preferences.

Testing and Analytics

As algorithms evolve, conduct A/B testing to understand how your content performs under different conditions. Utilize analytics tools provided by each platform to assess reach, engagement, and other relevant metrics. This data-driven approach empowers creators to make informed decisions and refine their strategies based on algorithmic insights.

4.2 Leveraging Algorithmic Trends to Boost Visibility
Rather than viewing algorithms as obstacles, content creators can strategically leverage algorithmic trends

to enhance their visibility and reach a broader audience.

Video Content Dominance

Many platforms prioritize video content due to its high engagement potential. Embrace this trend by incorporating more videos into your content strategy. Create engaging, short-form videos optimized for autoplay features and leverage platform-specific video tools like Instagram Reels or TikTok's Duet.

Timing and Frequency

Understanding the algorithm's preference for timing and frequency is crucial. Post when your audience is most active, as this increases the likelihood of your content appearing in their feeds. Consistent posting schedules also signal to algorithms that your account is active and worthy of visibility.

Utilizing New Features

Social media platforms regularly introduce new features to keep users engaged. Early adoption of these features often results in increased visibility, as platforms typically promote and prioritize content that utilizes new tools. Experiment with features like Instagram Guides, Twitter Spaces, or LinkedIn Stories to stay on the cutting edge.

4.3 Maximizing Reach and Engagement

Maximizing reach and engagement is at the core of successful social media monetization. By understanding how algorithms operate and strategically optimizing your content, you can foster a larger and more engaged audience.

Audience Engagement Tactics

Encourage audience engagement through interactive elements such as polls, quizzes, and questions. Platforms tend to boost content that generates more interaction. Respond promptly to comments, and ask open-ended questions to stimulate discussions. The more engagement your content receives, the higher its visibility in users' feeds.

Utilizing Hashtags Effectively

Hashtags play a crucial role in content discoverability. Research and use relevant and trending hashtags in your niche to increase the reach of your posts. Avoid overusing or spamming hashtags, as this can negatively impact your visibility. Tailor your hashtag strategy based on each platform's guidelines and trends.

Collaborating with Others

Algorithmic reach often extends when content creators collaborate. Partnering with others in your niche or industry can expose your content to a wider audience. Collaborations not only introduce your content to new followers but also signal to algorithms that your content is valuable and shareable.

Analytics and Iteration

Regularly analyze your content performance through platform analytics. Identify patterns related to the types of content that resonate most with your audience. Use this data to refine your content strategy, focusing on producing more of what works and adapting to algorithmic trends that contribute to increased reach and engagement.

In conclusion, mastering social media algorithms is an ongoing process that involves staying informed about updates, strategically leveraging algorithmic trends, and actively working to maximize reach and engagement. Content creators who adapt their strategies to align with algorithms are better positioned to navigate the dynamic landscape of social media, ultimately enhancing their opportunities for successful monetization.

Chapter 5: Growing Your Follower Base

In the world of social media monetization, the size and engagement level of your follower base are critical factors that directly impact your earning potential. This chapter explores effective growth hacking techniques, the importance of engaging with your audience to build a community, and the significance of analyzing metrics for continuous improvement to foster sustained and meaningful follower growth.

5.1 Implementing Effective Growth Hacking Techniques

Growing your follower base involves a combination of strategic planning, leveraging platform-specific features, and adopting growth hacking techniques that optimize your visibility.

Strategic Content Calendar

Develop a strategic content calendar that aligns with your niche and audience interests. Consistency in posting, both in terms of timing and content quality, signals to algorithms that your account is active and relevant. Plan content that elicits engagement, such as Q&A sessions, polls, or behind-the-scenes glimpses.

Utilizing Hashtags Strategically

Hashtags are powerful tools for expanding your reach. Research and incorporate relevant, trending hashtags into your posts to increase discoverability. Experiment with a mix of broad and niche-specific hashtags to reach a wider audience while still targeting those interested in your particular niche.

Collaborative Giveaways and Contests

Collaborative giveaways and contests with other content creators or brands can exponentially boost your follower count. Require participants to follow all collaborating accounts for eligibility. The potential for gaining followers increases as participants engage with your content and share the giveaway, creating a ripple effect.

Cross-Promotions and Shoutouts

Engage in cross-promotions and shoutouts with other creators in your niche. Collaborate with influencers or accounts with a similar follower count to share each other's content. This mutually beneficial strategy introduces your profile to a new audience, increasing the likelihood of gaining followers interested in your content.

5.2 Engaging with Your Audience: Building a Community

Building a community around your content is more than just accumulating followers; it's about fostering meaningful connections, interactions, and a sense of belonging.

Responding to Comments and Direct Messages

Engage actively with your audience by responding to comments and direct messages. Acknowledge and appreciate positive comments, and address questions or concerns promptly. This not only strengthens your relationship with existing followers but also encourages more interactions, enhancing your content's visibility.

Hosting Live Sessions and Q&A

Live sessions, whether on Instagram, Facebook, or other platforms, offer a real-time connection with your audience. Host Q&A sessions, share insights, and respond to comments live. This interactive approach not only boosts engagement but also humanizes your online presence, making you more relatable to your audience.

Encouraging User-Generated Content

Encourage your followers to create and share content related to your niche. Feature user-generated content on your profile, giving credit to the creators. This not only provides valuable social proof but also fosters a sense of community, where followers actively contribute to the content ecosystem.

Creating Exclusive Memberships or Groups

Platforms like Patreon or Facebook Groups allow you to create exclusive spaces for your most dedicated followers. Offer special content, behind-the-scenes access, or direct interactions in these spaces. Exclusive memberships strengthen the sense of community, providing additional value to those who choose to support you.

5.3 Analyzing Metrics for Continuous Improvement

To sustain follower growth, it's essential to continually analyze metrics, gaining insights into what works and making data-driven decisions for continuous improvement.

Tracking Follower Growth and Engagement

Utilize platform analytics to track your follower growth over time. Monitor engagement metrics, including likes, comments, and shares. Identify patterns related to the type of content that resonates most with your audience. This information guides your content strategy for future posts.

Audience Demographics and Preferences

Analyze audience demographics and preferences through platform insights. Understand the age, location, and interests of your followers. Tailor your content to align with these demographics, ensuring that your posts cater to the specific needs and preferences of your audience.

A/B Testing for Content Optimization

Conduct A/B testing to optimize content performance. Experiment with different post formats, captions, or posting times. Analyze the results to determine which variables contribute to increased engagement and follower growth. Continuously refine your strategy based on these findings.

Identifying Trends and Adaptation

Stay attuned to trends within your niche and adapt your content accordingly. Leverage popular trends, challenges, or relevant topics to stay current and maintain audience interest. Social media is dynamic, and being flexible in your approach ensures that your content remains engaging and shareable.

Chapter 6: Monetizing Content through Ads

Monetizing content through ads is a cornerstone of social media revenue generation. In this chapter, we will explore the intricacies of ad monetization, including understanding key ad platforms like Instagram, Facebook, and TikTok, optimizing ad placement and frequency for maximum impact, and utilizing A/B testing to continuously improve ad performance.

6.1 Understanding Ad Platforms: Instagram, Facebook, and TikTok

Each social media platform has its unique ad ecosystem, and understanding the nuances of these platforms is vital for effective monetization.

Instagram Ads

Instagram offers a diverse range of ad formats, including photo ads, video ads, carousel ads, and story ads. Leveraging the visual nature of Instagram, content creators can create visually stunning ads that seamlessly blend with organic content. Utilize Instagram's targeting options to reach specific demographics, interests, and behaviors, maximizing the relevance of your ads.

Facebook Ads

As the parent company of Instagram, Facebook provides a comprehensive ad platform with a wide range of targeting options. Content creators can create ads tailored to different objectives, including awareness, consideration, and conversion. Facebook's robust analytics tools enable precise tracking of ad performance, allowing for data-driven optimizations.

TikTok Ads

TikTok's ad platform is known for its immersive and engaging ad experiences. With options like in-feed ads, branded hashtag challenges, and branded effects, content creators can leverage the creativity and virality that characterize TikTok content. Understanding TikTok's younger demographic and the platform's emphasis on authenticity is key for crafting ads that resonate.

6.2 Optimizing Ad Placement and Frequency

Optimizing ad placement and frequency is crucial for striking a balance between generating revenue and maintaining a positive user experience.

Native Integration

Integrate ads seamlessly into the native user experience. Native ads feel less intrusive and more organic, enhancing the overall user experience. Match the aesthetics and style of your ads to the surrounding content, ensuring that they do not disrupt the flow of the user's engagement with the platform.

Strategic Placement

Identify strategic ad placements that align with user behavior. For instance, on Instagram, placing ads in Stories capitalizes on the high engagement rates within this format. On Facebook, considering the placement of ads in the news feed or right column depends on the campaign's objectives. Tailor ad placement to match the natural flow of user interactions.

Frequency Capping

Carefully manage ad frequency to avoid ad fatigue. Bombarding users with the same ad repeatedly can lead to disengagement and negative perceptions. Implement frequency capping to control the number of times an individual user sees the same ad within a specific time frame. This ensures that your ads remain impactful without becoming intrusive.

6.3 A/B Testing for Ad Performance Improvement

A/B testing is a powerful tool for refining ad performance and maximizing the return on investment. By systematically testing variations of ads, content creators can gain insights into what resonates best with their audience.

Testing Ad Copy and Creatives

Experiment with different ad copies and creatives to identify what captures the audience's attention. Test variations in headlines, descriptions, images, or videos to pinpoint the elements that drive better engagement and conversions. A/B testing provides valuable data to inform future ad content.

Ad Targeting Experiments

Refine your ad targeting through A/B testing. Test different audience segments based on demographics, interests, or behaviors to determine which segments yield the best results. This iterative process allows content creators to optimize their target audience, ensuring that ads reach the most receptive viewers.

Testing Call-to-Action (CTA)

The effectiveness of a call-to-action (CTA) can significantly impact ad performance. A/B test different CTAs to understand which prompts drive the desired user actions. Whether it's encouraging clicks, sign-ups, or purchases, refining the language and presentation of CTAs through testing can lead to increased conversion rates.

Performance Metrics Analysis

Regularly analyze key performance metrics such as click-through rates (CTR), conversion rates, and engagement rates. Identify trends and patterns in the data generated from A/B testing. This ongoing analysis informs strategic decisions, allowing content creators to allocate resources to the most effective ad variations.

In conclusion, monetizing content through ads requires a deep understanding of ad platforms, strategic optimization of ad placement and frequency, and a commitment to continuous improvement through A/B testing. As content creators navigate the dynamic landscape of social media, mastering the art of ad monetization ensures not only revenue generation but also a positive and engaging user experience.

Chapter 7: Harnessing the Power of Affiliate Marketing

Affiliate marketing stands as a potent avenue for content creators to diversify their income streams and maximize their earning potential. This chapter will delve into the intricacies of affiliate marketing, providing insights into identifying profitable affiliate programs, creating compelling affiliate content, and the essential aspect of tracking and analyzing affiliate conversions.

7.1 Identifying Profitable Affiliate Programs

The success of affiliate marketing begins with the careful selection of profitable affiliate programs. Consider the following strategies when identifying programs that align with your niche and audience:

Relevance to Your Niche

Choose affiliate programs that seamlessly integrate with your content and resonate with your audience's interests. Relevance is paramount – your audience is more likely to engage with affiliate products or services that complement the content they already enjoy.

High Commission Rates

Evaluate the commission rates offered by affiliate programs. While high rates may be enticing, also consider the product's price point and the likelihood of conversion. A balance between a competitive commission and the product's appeal to your audience ensures a mutually beneficial partnership.

Program Reputation and Trustworthiness

Research the reputation and trustworthiness of affiliate programs before committing. Read reviews, check for testimonials, and assess the program's track record. Trustworthy programs provide transparent tracking, timely payments, and reliable support, contributing to a positive affiliate marketing experience.

Cookie Duration and Attribution Models

Understand the cookie duration and attribution models of affiliate programs. A longer cookie duration increases the likelihood of earning commissions, allowing users more time to make a purchase after clicking the affiliate link. Additionally, be aware of attribution models, as they determine how conversions are credited to affiliates.

7.2 Creating Compelling Affiliate Content

Creating compelling affiliate content is an art that involves seamlessly integrating promotional elements into your regular content while maintaining authenticity and providing value to your audience.

Storytelling and Personal Experience

Craft narratives around affiliate products by incorporating storytelling and personal experiences. Share how the product or service has positively impacted your life, addressing pain points or providing solutions. Authenticity builds trust and resonates with your audience, making them more receptive to affiliate recommendations.

In-Depth Reviews and Tutorials

Provide comprehensive reviews and tutorials for affiliate products. Dive into the features, benefits, and potential drawbacks. Demonstrating how to use the product through tutorials or walkthroughs offers valuable insights to your audience, aiding in their decision-making process and increasing the likelihood of conversions.

Visual Appeal with Multimedia

Enhance the visual appeal of your affiliate content with multimedia elements. Utilize high-quality images, videos, or infographics to showcase the product in action. Visual content not only captures attention but also provides a more immersive experience, aiding in conveying the value of the affiliate offering.

Exclusive Deals and Bonuses

Negotiate exclusive deals or bonuses for your audience to incentivize conversions. Exclusive discounts, limited-time offers, or additional perks create a sense of urgency and exclusivity, encouraging your audience to take action. Clearly communicate these special arrangements in your affiliate content.

7.3 Tracking and Analyzing Affiliate Conversions

Tracking and analyzing affiliate conversions are pivotal steps in gauging the effectiveness of your affiliate marketing efforts and optimizing for better results.

Utilizing Tracking Tools

Leverage tracking tools provided by affiliate programs or third-party platforms to monitor the performance of your affiliate links. Track key metrics such as clicks, conversions, and commissions earned. These tools offer valuable insights into user behavior and the success of your promotional efforts.

Monitoring Conversion Funnels

Understand the conversion funnel for affiliate products. Analyze the user journey from clicking the affiliate link to completing the desired action, whether it's making a purchase or signing up. Identify potential drop-off points in the funnel and optimize your content or promotional strategies accordingly.

Split Testing for Optimization

Implement split testing, also known as A/B testing, to optimize your affiliate content. Test different variations of your content, such as headlines, calls-to-action, or visuals, to determine which elements contribute most to conversions. This iterative approach allows you to refine your strategies based on data-driven insights.

Assessing ROI and Performance

Regularly assess the return on investment (ROI) and overall performance of your affiliate marketing campaigns. Calculate the ratio of earnings to expenses, including any promotional or advertising costs. Understanding the financial impact of your efforts helps in prioritizing high-performing affiliate programs and optimizing your overall monetization strategy.

Chapter 8: Securing Lucrative Sponsorships

In the dynamic realm of social media monetization, securing lucrative sponsorships stands as a pinnacle achievement for content creators. This chapter explores the strategic steps involved in building a pitch-perfect sponsorship proposal, negotiating sponsorship deals and contracts, and maintaining positive, enduring relationships with sponsors.

8.1 Building a Pitch-Perfect Sponsorship Proposal

A compelling sponsorship proposal serves as the linchpin for attracting potential sponsors and showcasing the value you can offer. Craft a pitch-perfect sponsorship proposal using the following strategies:

Know Your Audience and Niche

Start by demonstrating a deep understanding of your audience and niche. Highlight key demographics, engagement metrics, and the unique aspects that set your content apart. Sponsors are drawn to influencers who can provide access to a specific and engaged target audience.

Showcase Your Reach and Engagement

Quantify your reach and engagement metrics to showcase the potential exposure sponsors can gain. Include statistics such as followers, average engagement rates, and demographic insights. Platforms like Instagram and YouTube offer analytics tools that can provide detailed insights into your audience's behavior.

Highlight Past Successful Campaigns

If applicable, showcase past successful sponsorship campaigns. Share case studies or testimonials from previous sponsors, emphasizing the positive outcomes and impact of your collaboration. This not only serves as a testament to your effectiveness but also instills confidence in potential sponsors.

Tailor Proposals to Each Sponsor

Customize your sponsorship proposals for each potential sponsor. Demonstrate a genuine interest in the brand by aligning your proposal with their values, products, or services. Highlight how your collaboration can enhance their marketing goals and resonate with your audience.

8.2 Negotiating Sponsorship Deals and Contracts

Negotiating sponsorship deals is an art that involves finding a mutually beneficial arrangement. Navigate this process effectively using the following tactics:

Clearly Define Deliverables

Be explicit about the deliverables you can provide. Clearly outline the type and frequency of content, whether it's sponsored posts, reviews, or dedicated videos. Specify the platforms and formats you'll utilize to maximize visibility. Clarity in deliverables sets expectations for both parties.

Determine Compensation Structures

Explore various compensation structures, including flat fees, commission-based models, or a combination of both. Consider the value you bring to the sponsor, your audience's responsiveness, and the effort required for the collaboration. Negotiate compensation that reflects the unique strengths of your content and audience.

Establish Timelines and Deadlines

Set clear timelines and deadlines for sponsored campaigns. Clearly articulate the start and end dates, as well as any intermediate milestones. Aligning on a schedule ensures that both parties are on the same page regarding the campaign's duration and the expected delivery of content.

Include Legal Considerations

Incorporate legal considerations into sponsorship agreements. Address issues such as exclusivity, usage rights, and disclosure requirements. Clearly define how sponsored content will be used, whether the sponsor has exclusive rights, and how disclosures will be handled to comply with relevant regulations.

8.3 Maintaining Positive Relationships with Sponsors

Building and maintaining positive relationships with sponsors is essential for long-term success in the world of social media monetization. Follow these strategies to cultivate positive and enduring sponsor relationships:

Communicate Transparently

Foster open and transparent communication with sponsors. Keep them informed about campaign progress, any challenges faced, and proactive solutions you are implementing. Timely and honest communication builds trust and demonstrates your commitment to the success of the collaboration.

Over-Deliver on Expectations

Go above and beyond to over-deliver on the agreed-upon expectations. Exceeding sponsor expectations not only enhances the success of the current campaign but also positions you favorably for future collaborations. Consider adding extra value, such as bonus content or extended promotion periods.

Provide Detailed Analytics and Reports

Offer detailed analytics and reports showcasing the performance of sponsored campaigns. Share metrics such as reach, engagement, and conversion rates. Demonstrating the impact of the collaboration provides sponsors with valuable insights and reinforces the value of their investment.

Seek Feedback and Iterate

Actively seek feedback from sponsors after campaigns conclude. Understand their perspective on what worked well and areas for improvement. Use this feedback as a learning opportunity to refine your approach and enhance the effectiveness of future collaborations.

Cultivate Long-Term Partnerships

Strive to cultivate long-term partnerships with sponsors. Building enduring relationships allows for repeat collaborations, potentially at higher compensation levels. As sponsors witness the consistent positive results of your campaigns, they are more likely to view you as a valuable, trusted partner.

Chapter 9: Diversifying Income Streams

In the dynamic landscape of social media monetization, content creators are increasingly recognizing the importance of diversifying income streams. This chapter delves into three key strategies for diversification: exploring e-commerce opportunities, launching digital products such as courses, ebooks, and merchandise, and monetizing exclusive memberships and subscriptions.

9.1 Exploring E-commerce Opportunities

E-commerce presents a lucrative avenue for content creators to monetize their influence by offering physical products related to their niche or personal brand. Consider the following steps when exploring e-commerce opportunities:

Niche-Relevant Products

Identify products that align with your niche and resonate with your audience. This could include custom-designed merchandise, specialty items, or even collaborations with other brands. Ensure that the products you choose enhance your brand image and offer value to your followers.

Print-on-Demand Services

Explore print-on-demand services that allow you to create and sell custom-designed products without the need for inventory management. Platforms like Printful, Printify, or Teespring enable content creators to design and sell products like T-shirts, mugs, and phone cases, with the fulfillment handled by the service.

E-commerce Platforms Integration

Consider integrating e-commerce features directly into your social media platforms. Platforms like Instagram and Facebook offer built-in shopping functionalities that enable followers to browse and purchase products seamlessly. Utilize these features to streamline the purchasing process and increase conversion rates.

Limited Edition or Exclusive Drops

Create a sense of exclusivity and urgency by introducing limited edition or exclusive product drops. Announce these releases to your audience, generating anticipation and excitement. Limited availability encourages swift purchases, fostering a sense of exclusivity for those who acquire the products.

9.2 Launching Digital Products: Courses, Ebooks, and Merchandise

Digital products offer content creators an additional avenue for monetization, allowing them to share their expertise, knowledge, and creativity with their audience. Here's how to successfully launch digital products:

Online Courses

Leverage your expertise by creating and selling online courses. Identify topics within your niche that align with your knowledge and audience interests. Platforms like Teachable, Udemy, or Skillshare provide tools for content creators to structure, market, and sell their courses to a global audience.

Ebooks and Guides

Compile your insights, experiences, or expertise into ebooks or guides. Self-publishing platforms like Amazon Kindle Direct Publishing or Gumroad enable you to publish and sell digital books. Design visually appealing covers and market your ebooks to your audience, offering valuable content in a convenient format.

Exclusive Merchandise

Extend your merchandise offerings into the digital realm by creating exclusive digital products. This could include digital art, wallpapers, or even exclusive access to online events or Q&A sessions. Platforms like Patreon or your own website can facilitate the sale and distribution of these digital offerings.

Bundled Product Packages

Create bundled packages that combine various digital products. For instance, offer a package that includes an ebook, an online course, and exclusive digital merchandise at a discounted rate. Bundling products provides added value for your audience and encourages them to invest in a comprehensive content package.

9.3 Monetizing Exclusive Memberships and Subscriptions

Exclusive memberships and subscription models provide content creators with recurring revenue while offering unique benefits to dedicated followers. Here's how to effectively monetize exclusive memberships and subscriptions:

Patreon and Membership Platforms

Leverage platforms like Patreon, Buy Me a Coffee, or YouTube Memberships to create exclusive membership tiers. Offer tier-specific benefits such as access to premium content, early access to videos, exclusive behind-the-scenes footage, or personalized shoutouts. Encourage your audience to support you on an ongoing basis.

Subscription-Based Content

Consider creating a subscription-based model for premium content. Platforms like Substack, for written content, or OnlyFans, for various types of content, allow content creators to charge a monthly subscription fee for exclusive access. Clearly communicate the value subscribers will receive to incentivize sign-ups.

Virtual Events and Community Building

Organize virtual events and community-building activities exclusively for your members or subscribers. This could include live Q&A sessions, virtual meet-ups, or members-only forums. Fostering a sense of community enhances the perceived value of exclusive memberships and encourages retention.

Regularly Deliver Exclusive Content

Consistently deliver exclusive content to your members or subscribers. Whether it's monthly newsletters, exclusive videos, or members-only discounts, regularly providing valuable content reinforces the benefits of being part of the exclusive community. Regular engagement contributes to long-term subscriber satisfaction.

Chapter 10: Legal and Ethical Considerations

As content creators navigate the expansive world of social media monetization, understanding and adhering to legal and ethical considerations become paramount. This chapter will delve into key aspects including understanding copyright and intellectual property, disclosing sponsored content, and complying with regulations, as well as handling disputes and protecting your online reputation.

10.1 Understanding Copyright and Intellectual Property

Respect for Intellectual Property

Respecting intellectual property is fundamental for content creators. Understand the distinction between original content creation and potential copyright infringement. Always seek permission or provide proper attribution when using someone else's work, whether it's images, music, or any other creative material.

Licensing and Usage Rights

Familiarize yourself with licensing and usage rights associated with creative assets. Some content may be available under specific licenses that dictate how it can be used. Ensure compliance with these licenses and avoid using content in a manner that exceeds the permitted usage rights.

Safeguarding Your Own Content

Protect your own content by clearly defining usage rights and licenses for your audience. Consider watermarks or other protective measures for visual content. When collaborating with others, establish agreements regarding the use and attribution of shared content to avoid potential disputes.

Trademark Considerations

Be aware of trademark considerations when incorporating brand names or logos into your content. Unauthorized use of trademarks can lead to legal consequences. Understand the trademark status of brands you mention or feature in your content and, when in doubt, seek legal advice.

10.2 Disclosing Sponsored Content and Complying with Regulations

Transparent Disclosure

Maintain transparency by clearly disclosing sponsored content to your audience. Clearly label posts, videos, or other content that involves a financial exchange or partnership with a brand. This transparency not only builds trust with your audience but also helps you comply with regulatory requirements.

FTC Guidelines in the United States

If you operate within the United States, familiarize yourself with the Federal Trade Commission (FTC) guidelines for endorsements and sponsored content. The FTC requires clear and conspicuous disclosure of any material connection between influencers and brands. Understand the specific disclosure requirements and integrate them into your content.

Compliance with Local Regulations

Recognize that disclosure requirements may vary across different countries and regions. Stay informed about local regulations regarding sponsored content and endorsements. Some regions may have specific guidelines or authorities overseeing influencer marketing practices.

Ethical Considerations in Endorsements

Maintain ethical standards in your endorsements. Only promote products or services that align with your values and that you genuinely believe in. Misleading endorsements or false claims can not only harm your reputation but may also lead to legal consequences.

10.3 Handling Disputes and Protecting Your Online Reputation

Clear Agreements and Contracts

When entering into collaborations, establish clear agreements and contracts with brands or partners. Clearly define expectations, deliverables, compensation, and any usage rights. Having a well-documented agreement can serve as a reference in case of disputes and provides a foundation for legal recourse if necessary.

Dispute Resolution Mechanisms

Incorporate dispute resolution mechanisms into your agreements. Outline steps for resolving conflicts or disagreements amicably before resorting to legal action. Mediation or alternative dispute resolution processes can be more efficient and cost-effective than engaging in lengthy legal battles.

Online Reputation Management

Prioritize the protection of your online reputation. Respond professionally to criticism or negative feedback. Address issues promptly and transparently. A thoughtful and constructive response to criticism can mitigate potential reputational damage and demonstrate your commitment to accountability and improvement.

Seek Legal Advice When Necessary

When faced with legal uncertainties or disputes, seek professional legal advice. Consulting with an attorney who specializes in influencer marketing or intellectual property law can provide guidance tailored to your specific situation. Legal counsel can help you navigate complex issues and make informed decisions.

Periodic Legal Audits

Conduct periodic legal audits of your content and collaborations. Regularly review and update your agreements, disclosures, and compliance measures to align with evolving legal standards. Staying proactive in legal matters helps prevent potential issues before they escalate.

In conclusion, as content creators engage in social media monetization, understanding and adhering to legal and ethical considerations are integral to long-term success. By prioritizing respect for intellectual property, transparently disclosing sponsored content, and implementing effective mechanisms for dispute resolution and reputation protection, content creators can build a foundation of trust with their audience and establish a resilient and ethical online presence.

Chapter 11: Overcoming Challenges in Social Media Monetization

Social media monetization, while promising significant opportunities, is not without its challenges. Content creators often encounter obstacles ranging from algorithm changes to burnout. This chapter explores strategies for overcoming these challenges, including dealing with algorithm changes and platform updates, managing burnout, and adapting to industry shifts and emerging trends.

11.1 Dealing with Algorithm Changes and Platform Updates

Stay Informed and Adaptive

Algorithm changes and platform updates are inherent in the fast-paced world of social media. Stay informed about changes on the platforms you utilize. Follow official updates, blogs, or forums where changes are discussed. Being adaptive and quick to understand and implement new features can give you a competitive edge.

Diversify Platform Presence

Relying solely on one platform can leave you vulnerable to the impact of algorithm changes. Diversify your presence across multiple platforms to spread risk. By building a multi-platform strategy, you create a more stable and resilient online presence.

Build Strong Community Engagement

Algorithm changes often prioritize content that fosters high engagement. Focus on building a strong community that actively engages with your content. Respond to comments, foster discussions, and encourage audience participation. Strong community engagement not only benefits your algorithmic visibility but also creates a loyal follower base.

Analyze and Adjust Strategy

Regularly analyze the performance of your content post-algorithm changes. Use platform analytics to understand how your content is being received. If necessary, adjust your content strategy, posting schedule, or engagement tactics based on the insights gathered. The ability to adapt quickly is crucial in the face of evolving algorithms.

11.2 Managing Burnout and Maintaining Consistency

Set Realistic Goals and Boundaries

Burnout is a real concern in the world of content creation. Set realistic goals and boundaries for yourself. Understand your capacity for content creation, engagement, and collaboration. Establishing clear limits helps in preventing burnout and maintaining long-term consistency.

Develop a Content Calendar

Create a content calendar to plan and organize your content in advance. Having a structured schedule reduces the stress of last-minute content creation. It also ensures a consistent flow of content for your audience, helping you stay active without feeling overwhelmed.

Delegate or Outsource Tasks

Consider delegating or outsourcing certain tasks to manage workload effectively. Whether it's editing, graphic design, or administrative tasks, bringing in support allows you to focus on the aspects of content creation that align with your strengths and interests.

Prioritize Self-Care

Prioritize self-care to prevent burnout. Schedule breaks, maintain a healthy work-life balance, and engage in activities outside of content creation. A well-rested and balanced creator is more likely to produce high-quality content consistently.

11.3 Adapting to Industry Shifts and Emerging Trends

Stay Ahead of Trends

The digital landscape evolves rapidly with emerging trends and shifts in user behavior. Stay ahead of industry trends by actively monitoring your niche, attending relevant conferences, and engaging in online communities. Being an early adopter of emerging trends positions you as a trendsetter and can attract new followers.

Experiment with New Content Formats

Experimenting with new content formats can help you stay relevant and appealing to your audience. Explore video content, live streams, interactive features, or emerging social media platforms. Adapting to the changing preferences of your audience can enhance your visibility and engagement.

Network and Collaborate

Engage in networking and collaborations within your industry. Building connections with other content creators, brands, and influencers opens doors to new opportunities and insights. Collaborations can introduce your content to new audiences and provide exposure in different circles.

Diversify Monetization Strategies

Diversifying your monetization strategies is crucial in adapting to industry shifts. Explore new revenue streams, such as exclusive memberships, virtual events, or affiliate marketing. A diversified approach ensures that you are not overly dependent on a single source of income, making your monetization strategy more resilient.

Monitor Analytics and Feedback

Regularly monitor analytics and gather feedback to gauge the reception of your content and strategies. Pay attention to metrics such as engagement rates, follower growth, and audience demographics. Analyzing data allows you to identify successful strategies and areas for improvement, guiding your adaptation to industry shifts.

In conclusion, overcoming challenges in social media monetization requires a combination of adaptability, strategic planning, and self-care. By staying informed about algorithm changes, managing burnout, and proactively adapting to industry shifts, content creators can navigate the evolving landscape with resilience and success.

Chapter 12: Future Trends in Social Media Monetization

Embarking on the journey of social media monetization is not merely a pursuit of the present but a voyage into the boundless possibilities that the future holds. In this final chapter, we set our sights on the inspiring prospects that await content creators, entrepreneurs, and visionaries in the dynamic realm of social media monetization.

12.1 Predicting the Next Wave of Social Media Platforms

As we stand at the cusp of the future, predicting the next wave of social media platforms becomes an exhilarating exercise. The digital landscape is ever-evolving, birthing new platforms that redefine how content is created, consumed, and monetized.

Keep a watchful eye on emerging platforms, those that resonate with niche audiences, and platforms that pioneer innovative features.

Niches Beyond the Mainstream

The future might unveil social media platforms catering to specific niches, fostering communities with shared interests and passions. These platforms could offer tailored monetization features, creating opportunities for content creators to thrive in more specialized spaces.

Augmented Reality and Virtual Reality Integration

Anticipate the integration of augmented reality (AR) and virtual reality (VR) into social media platforms. Immersive experiences that blend the digital and physical worlds can open up novel avenues for content creation and monetization. Explore how AR filters, virtual events, and interactive experiences can be harnessed for both engagement and revenue.

Decentralized and Blockchain-Based Platforms

The rise of decentralized platforms and blockchain technology may redefine how content creators interact with their audience and monetize their work. Smart contracts, non-fungible tokens (NFTs), and decentralized finance (DeFi) could introduce new, decentralized revenue streams and ownership models.

12.2 Embracing Technological Innovations for Monetization

Technological innovations are the heartbeat of progress, and content creators must not merely adapt but actively embrace these innovations to fuel their journey toward monetization excellence.

Artificial Intelligence for Content Personalization

The integration of artificial intelligence (AI) in social media platforms is set to revolutionize content personalization. Imagine an AI-driven algorithm that tailors content recommendations based on individual preferences, optimizing not only user engagement but also providing new avenues for targeted monetization.

Interactive and Shoppable Content

The future heralds an era of interactive and shoppable content. Explore features that allow your audience to directly engage with and purchase products showcased in your content. Augmenting your content with interactive elements and direct purchasing capabilities can elevate the user experience while creating additional revenue streams.

Voice and Audio Monetization

With the surge in popularity of voice-based interactions and audio content, anticipate monetization opportunities in the realm of podcasts, voice-activated ads, and interactive audio experiences. As voice technology evolves, consider how your content can leverage these advancements for both engagement and revenue generation.

12.3 Staying Ahead in the Ever-Evolving Landscape of Social Media Monetization

Staying ahead in the ever-evolving landscape of social media monetization requires a blend of foresight, adaptability, and a passion for innovation. Let the future be a canvas on which you paint your success story.

Lifelong Learning and Skill Development

Commit to lifelong learning and continuous skill development. The landscape of social media and digital marketing is a dynamic tapestry that demands constant evolution. Stay abreast of emerging technologies, trends, and industry insights to position yourself as a pioneer in the evolving monetization landscape.

Collaboration and Community Building

Embrace collaboration as a catalyst for growth. In the future, community building and cross-platform collaborations will play a pivotal role in expanding your reach and diversifying your monetization strategies. Forge meaningful connections with fellow creators, brands, and your audience to create a resilient ecosystem.

Purpose-Driven Content Creation

As the future unfolds, infuse purpose into your content creation. Audiences are increasingly drawn to content that aligns with values, social causes, and authenticity. Create content with a purpose, one that resonates with your audience and provides them with a meaningful and enriching experience.

Agile Strategy and Adaptability

Cultivate an agile strategy that embraces change and adaptability. The future of social media monetization will undoubtedly bring unforeseen challenges and opportunities. Be ready to pivot, experiment, and iterate on your strategies as you navigate the ever-shifting currents of the digital landscape.

As you embark on this inspiring journey into the future of social media monetization, remember that you are not merely a participant but a visionary shaping the narrative. Embrace the unknown with enthusiasm, innovate with purpose, and let your passion for creating and monetizing content be the guiding light toward a future filled with endless possibilities. May your journey be as remarkable as the impact you make on the digital horizon.